ek 12.1.88

ORDER NO 22511   PAI 89/NF   253

**

PLUCKROSE, Henry
Weight. Lond., Watts, 1987. (Knowabout) 26p.
ISBN 0 86313 510 2   hbk $14.95

See annotation for *Counting*. Provides basic information about comparing
weights in everyday situations. K/Lower.

ORDER NO 2248   PAI 89/NF   250

**

PLUCKROSE, Henry
Counting. Lond., Watts, 1987. (Knowabout) 26p.
ISBN 0 86313 506 4   hbk $14.95

This and the following three titles present clear explanations of mathematics
topics to Lower school students. Each title is imaginative in its presentation and
provides an interactive approach to the subject. Excellent for encouraging
children to search for and explore mathematical concepts within their environ-
ment. Crisp colour photographs dominate each page and reinforce the textual
information. K/Lower.

KNOWABOUT
Weight

KNOWABOUT
Weight

Text: Henry Pluckrose
Photography: Chris Fairclough

Franklin Watts
London/New York/Sydney/Toronto

© 1987 Franklin Watts
12a Golden Square
London W1

ISBN: 0 86313 510 2

Editor: Ruth Thomson
Design: Edward Kinsey
Additional photographs: Zefa,
The Zoological Society of London

Typesetting: Keyspools Limited

Printed in Hong Kong

About this book

This book is designed for use in the home, playgroup and infant school.

Mathematics is part of the child's world. It is not just about interpreting numbers or in mastering the tricks of addition or multiplication. Mathematics is about *Ideas*. These ideas (or concepts) have been developed over the centuries to help explain particular qualities, such as size, weight, height, as well as relationships and comparisons. Yet all too often the important part which an understanding of mathematics will play in a child's development is forgotten or ignored.

Most adults can solve simple mathematical tasks by "doing them in their head". For example you can probably add up or subtract simple numbers without the need for counters, beads or fingers. Young children find such abstractions almost impossible to master. They need to see, talk, touch and experiment.

The photographs in this book and the text which supports them have been prepared with one major aim. They have been chosen to encourage talk around topics which are essentially mathematical. By talking with you, the young reader will be helped to explore some of the central concepts which underpin mathematics. It is upon an understanding of these concepts that a child's future mastery of mathematics will be built.

Have you ever weighed yourself?
What did you weigh?
What does the word 'weigh' mean?

Weight is a measuring word.
We weigh things to find out
how heavy they are.

Why do we need to measure weight?

We need to measure
the right amount of flour to put in a cake.

The same amount of flour must be put in each sack.

Everything weighs something.
Even very light things have weight.

The feather weighs less
than the stone.

How does this picture show
that the stone is heavier
than the feather?

We can guess about the weight
of some things.
We can guess that the toy car
weighs less than the wheel.

We know that the girl could not lift a real bear like this!

Guessing that one thing is heavier
than another is not always easy.

How could we find out
which of these two piles
is the heavier?

We could weigh them.

Which is heavier?
Which is lighter?

Could you guess
which of these two things
is the heavier?

Was your guess right?

Weights like these are used
to measure heaviness.

A kilogram of apples will weigh
exactly the same
wherever it is bought.

If the apples were heavier
than a kilogram,
the scales would not balance.

If the apples were lighter
than a kilogram,
the scales would not balance either.

By using weights, like the gram
and the kilogram, we can compare
the weights of different things.

The kilogram of apples . . .

is as heavy as a kilogram of stones.

Would a kilogram of flour
weigh more, less or the same
as a kilogram of feathers?

It can be useful
and important
to weigh things.

Doctors weigh babies
to check
that they are growing
properly.

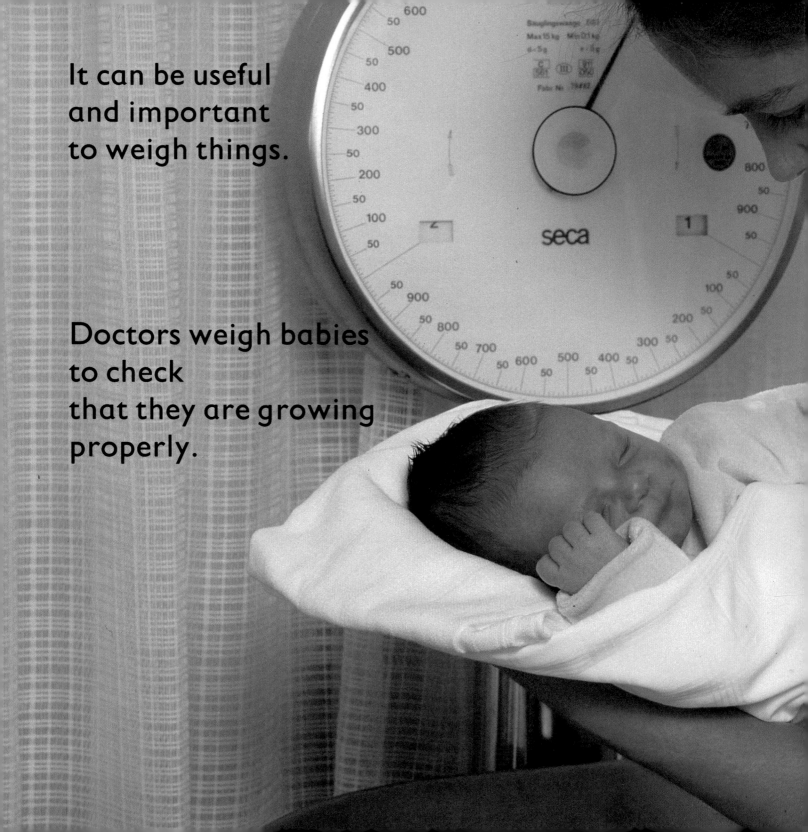

Even elephants need
to be weighed sometimes.

Luggage is weighed at the airport before it goes on a plane.

Shopkeepers weigh fruit and vegetables, so that you know how much they will cost.

Experiment for yourself.
Find a balance, some weights
and some sand.

Can you make the two pans balance?